STARTING FROM SAN FRANCISCO

LAWRENCE FERLINGHETTI

A NEW DIRECTIONS PAPERBOOK

Some of the poems in this book have been published in the following magazines, to which grateful acknowledgment for permission to reprint is here given: *Beatitude, Between Worlds, Big Table, Evergreen Review, New Directions 17, New Directions 19, The Outsider.*

The Eisenhower and Berlin poems were first published as broadsides by Golden Mountain Press, and the Castro poem as a broadside by City Lights Books, though the Berlin poem was somewhat revised for this book.

Published simultaneously in Canada by
Penguin Books Canada Limited.
Manufactured in the United States of America.

New Directions Books are printed in acid-free paper.

New Directions Books are published for James Laughlin
by New Directions Publishing Corporation,
80 Eighth Avenue, New York 10011.

EIGHTH PRINTING

CONTENTS

To PHILLIPS RUSSELL, professor emeritus,
in return for some seeds
he perhaps didn't know he sowed

STARTING FROM SAN FRANCISCO

Here I go again
crossing the country in coach trains
(back to my old
lone wandering)
All night Eastward . . . Upward
over the Great Divide and on
into Utah
over Great Salt Plain
and onward, rocking,
the white dawn burst
across mesas,
table-lands,
all flat, all laid away.
Great glary sun—
wood bridge over water. . . .
Later in still light, we still reel onward—
Onward?
Back and forth, across the Continent,
bang bang
by any wheel or horse,
any rail,
by car

by buggy
by stagecoach,
walking,
riding,
hooves pounding the Great Plains,
caravans into the night. Forever.
Into Wyoming.
All that day and night, rocking through it,
snow on steppes and plains of November,
roads lost in it—or never existent—
back in the beginning again, no People yet,
no ruts Westward yet
under the snow. . . .
Still more huge spaces we bowl through,
still untouched dark land—
Indomitable.
Horizons of mesas
like plains of Spain high up
in Don Quixote country—
sharp eroded towers of bluffs
like windmills tilted,
"los molinos" of earth, abandoned—
Great long rectangular stone islands
sticking up on far plains, like forts
or immense light cargo ships
high on plains of water,
becalmed and rudderless,
props thrashing wheat,
stranded forever,
no one on those bridges. . . .
Later again, much later,
one small halfass town,
followed by one telephone wire

and one straight single iron road
hung to the tracks as by magnets
attached to a single endless fence,
past solitary pumping stations,
each with a tank, a car, a small house, a dog,
no people anywhere—
All hiding?
White Man gone home?
Must be a cowboy someplace. . . .
Birds flap from fences, trestles,
caw and caw their nothingness.
Stone church sticks up
quote Out of Nowhere unquote
This must be Interzone
between Heaven and Brooklyn.
Do they have a Classified Section
as in phonebooks
in the back of the Bibles here?
Otherwise they'd never find Anything.
Try Instant Zen. . . .
Still later again,
sunset and strange clouds like udders
rayed with light from below—
some God's hand sticks through,
black trees stand out.
The world is a winter farm—
Cradle we rocked out of—
prairie schooners into Pullmans,
their bright saloons sheeted in oblivion—
Wagon-lits—bedwagons over the prairies,
bodies nested in them,
hurtled through night,
inscrutable. . . .

7

Onward still . . . or Backward . . .
huge snow fields still, on and on,
still no one,
Indians all gone to Florida
or Cuba!
Train hoots at something
in the nowhere we still rock through,
Dingding crossroads flicker by,
Mining towns, once roaring,
now shrunk to the railhead,
streetlights stoned with loneliness
or lit with leftover sun
they drank too much of during the day. . . .
And at long last now
this world shrunk
to one lone brakeman's face
stuck out of darkness—
long white forehead
like bleached skull of cow—
huge black sad eyes—
high-peaked cloth cap, grey-striped—
swings his railroad lantern high, close up,
as our window whizzes by—
his figure splashed upon it,
slanted, muezzin-like,
very grave, very tall,
strange skeleton—
Who stole America?

Myself I saw in the window reflected.

NEW YORK—
ALBANY

God i had forgotten how
the Hudson burns
in indian autumn
Saugerties
Coxsackie
fall away through
all those trees
The leaves die turning
falling fallen
falling into loam of dark
yellow into death
Disappearing
falling fallen falling
god god those
'pestilence-stricken multitudes'
rushed into the streets
blown all blasted
They are hurting them
with wood rakes
They are raking them
in great hills
They are burning them
lord lord
the leaves curl burning
the curled smoke gives up
to eternity
Never
never the same leaf turn again
the same leaves burn

lord lord
in a red field
a white stallion stands
and pees his oblivion
upon those leaves
washing my bus window
only now blacked out
by a covered bridge
we flash through
only once
No roundtrip ticket
Lord lord never returning
the youth years fallen
away back then
Under the Linden trees in Boston Common
Lord Lord
Trees think
through these woods of years
They flame forever
with those thoughts
Lord Lord
i did not see eternity
the other night
but now in burning
turning day
Lord Lord Lord
every bush burns
Love licks
all down
All gone
in the red end
Lord Lord Lord Lord
Small nuts fall
Mine too

EUPHORIA

As I approach the state of pure euphoria
    I find I need a largersize typewriter case
    to carry my underwear in
    and scars on my conscience
    are wounds imbedded in
    the gum eraser of my skin
    which still erases itself
As I approach the state of pure euphoria
    moon hides hot face in cool rice rain
    of Chinese painting
    and I cannot sleep because of the thunder
    under the summer afternoon
    in which a girl puts on a record of
    crazy attempts to play a saxophone
    punctuated by terrible forced laughter
    in another room
As I approach the state of pure euphoria
    they are building all the cities now
    on only one side of the street
    and my shoes walk up sides of buildings
    leaving tracks of windows
    with their soles of panes about to crack
    and shoe-tongues of roll-up shades alack
    I see my roll-up tongue upon a string
    and see my face upon the stick of it

as on a pendulum about to swing
a playing-card image with bound feet
an upside-down hanged Villon
And Mama recedes in a hand-held photo
and Dad is named Ludwig
in a lost real-estate project ended in water
Saratoga Avenue Yonkers
where I now hang and swing
on a last tree that stands drinking
and where I'd still sing partsongs
in a field of rapture
but an angel has me by the balls
and my castrato voice comes out too small
with a girl that puts a laughing record on
in another room
As I approach the state of pure euphoria
my eyes are gringo spies and I
may anytime be changed to birds
by a Tungus explosion that controls time
but I am no apocalyptic kid
and cannot sleep because of the thunder
under the summer afternoon
and my dumb bird's eye starts
out of my head
and flies around the world
in which a girl puts on
her record made of flesh
And I am animals without clothes
looking for a naked unity
but I'm divided up into countries
and I'm in Tibet on potato legs
and am a strange kind of clown
with befloured face and hair plastered down

and cannot sleep because of the thunder
under the needle my flesh turns under
She has turned it on
She has turned it over
She has turned me on
to play my other side
Her breasts bloom
figs burst
sun is white
I'll never come back
I wear Egyptian clothing

BIG FAT HAIRY VISION OF EVIL

I.

Evil evil evil evil
World is evil
Life is evil
All is evil
if i ride the horse of hate
with its evil hooded eye
turning world to evil
Evil is death warmed over
Evil is Live spelled backward
Evil is lamb burning bright
Evil is love fried upon a spit
and turned upon itself
Evil is sty in eye of universe
hung upon a coughing horse
that follows me at night
thru a hollow street
wearing blinders
Evil is green gloves inside out
next to a double martini
on a cocktail table
Evil is lush with horse teeth
Evil is running after me
with glue feet
i'm running
Evil is screwing strangers
after cocktail parties
Poor dear flesh not evil

Lonely meat not evil
But evil is gooking
in my window
i am paranoid about evil
Evil is forty years old
and in my wrong mind
Evil is being out of my head
asleep or awake
Evil passes blind
thru filtertips of mind
in pot visions
where a horse walks
a horse who wants to eat me
Horse eats consciousness
i am afraid of it
i am running
i hate you evil
mad horse
We all go mad
when we die
but to ride mad horse alive
is a form of dying
each mad day a death
i am paranoid about it
Evil is out to catch me
Horse is humping after me
wearing blinders
Horse wants me to mount
Horse wants me to ride
without a halter
i am running from it
with two feet
i'm afraid
i don't want to die

2.

Evil evil evil evil evil evil evil
even if three naked monkeys
see no hear no speak no evil
Ebony Buddha With Three Eyes
is evil to evil eyes
Bronze Image of Dancing Krishna
is evil
Tibetan Conquerer of Death
draped in human skin
is evil
Singing Bodhisattva
is evil
in evil eyes
All those broody figures
running after me
evil eyeballs
rolling after me
will catch up to me
stony flowers fall on me
if i don't watch out
Flowers aren't evil
but Power is evil
Captain Bigarini
with his sad sad salutes
is evil
Naked Lunch is evil lunch
because it is the brunch of hate
i am not ready to eat it
i am not that hungry
i am afraid
i cannot run forever
i'm a relay runner

with a hollow baton
with a screwy message in it
which i can't quite decipher
a strange message
an ecstatic message
in a hollow baton
shuttled thru the tubes of earth
A Paris pneumatique
lost in Macy's basement
i must not drop it and lose the message
which i've never been able to read
on the run
i'm still running with it
Horse still running behind
Horse will catch me in the living end
He'll lie down on top of me
in my horsehair grave
He will gnaw my lowest bone
with his dingbat teeth
He will stretch his legs along my limbs
to make me one with him
Horse will lick my horsy face
with his gluepot tongue
Horse will puke on me
Poop his baked potatoes out on me
in death's insanity
and i will eat that naked lunch
that turns me into him
in the death of that god
which is consciousness itself
Ah but i will not look out
before that date
thru Horse's fur windows
and vomit landscapes!

FLYING OUT OF IT

I fly and see America

is mad mother

is being transformed in fillingstations

is Lucky Louis in two shoes

is sad Murphy

I see Gloria without her girdle

Life is sad

I see we're all sane sober pure

made over into ourselves

I see a great age is coming

the great time

Boom Boom

No more

beautiful birches

white in the gloaming

heaven no rest home

among the galaxies

We're spinning

past it

Away
I'll climb over
Death swings
its dumb bell
I'll catch it
I fly no
white heliocopter of grace
and there's no chocolate yet
on sundaes
in the deep South
though naked mama blow a black trumpet
But still—
birds flute up here
Crow-caw cracks
the universe
Ah there's a slit
to slither through
into eternity
Look look
there's love
yes love
Ah love
cannot make it
Pied Piper's cave
clangs shut

HIDDEN DOOR

Hidden door dead secret
           which is Mother
Hidden door dead secret
           which is Father
Hidden door dead secret
           of our buried life
Hidden door behind which man carries
           his footprints along the streets
Hidden door of clay hands knocking
Hidden door without handles
           whose life is made of knocks
           by hand and foot
           Poor hand poor foot poor life!
Hidden door with hair for hinges
Hidden door with lips for latches
Hidden door with skeletons for keys
Hidden door autobiography of humanity
Hidden door dictionary of the universe
Hidden door palimpsest of myself
Hidden door I'm made of
           with my sticks of limbs
Hidden door pathetic fallacy
           of the evidence of the senses
           as to the nature of reality
Hidden door in blind eyes of termites
           that knock knock

Hidden door blind man with tin cup
        on a stone corner deaf and dumb
Hidden door train-whistle lost
        in book of night
Hidden door on night's wheels I blundering follow
        like a rhinoceros drinking through cities
Hidden door of carrier-pigeons' wings
        which have half-forgotten
        their destination
Hidden door plane's wing that skids in space
        casting stone shadow
        on sundial of earth
Hidden door flying boxcar of history
Hidden door of Christ's suicide
Hidden door of Sunday without church
Hidden door of animal faces animal laughter animal dreams
        and hidden door Cro-Magnon Man
        among machines
        and hidden door of his still uncollected
        Collective Unconscious
Hidden door on classroom blackboards
        all over Europe
Hidden door dark forest of America
        knock knock in North Dakota
Hidden door that wings over America
        and slants over San Francisco
        and slams into the Pacific
        drifting eternally southward
        to Tierra del Fuego
        with a knock knock undersea
        at lost door of Lota coal mines
Hidden door surfboard to lost shore of light
        and hidden door floated up on tides
        like a shipwrecked coffinlid

                    bearing blind mouths blind breasts blind thought
                    through the centuries
Hidden door sea-angel cast-up Albatross
                    spouting seasperm of love in thirty languages
                    and the love-ship of life
                    sunk by the poison-squid of hate
Hidden door double-winged sticky-bird plumed serpent
                    stuck to moon afire forever drunk in time
                    flapping loose in eternity
Hidden door of the future mystic life
                    among Magellan's nebulae
                    and hidden door of my mislaid
                    visionary self
Hidden door San Luis rope-bridge which is man
                    hung between nature and spirit
Hidden door of the spirit seen as a fleshy thing
                    and hidden door of eyes and vulvas
                    that still open only with a key
                    of cartilage and flesh
                    and hidden door frozen Inca mummy
                    Prince of the Plomo
                    fucked to death in sun-god sacrifice
Hidden door tin cup of blind brother mutes
                    crouched on a Cuzco corner
                    blowing bamboo flutes
                    at coca midnight
Hidden door of the Andes at ten thousand feet
                    in a ragged mist of ruins and red horizons
                    with a seacoast hung below
                    still lost among conquistadors
                    horses dogs and incomprehensible laws
Hidden door wild river of the Urubamba
                    upon which still floats somewhere
                    the lost herb that separates soul from body

and hidden door which is itself that herb
and hidden door which is that separation
and hidden door made of mirrors
on the waters of this river
in which I cannot see beyond myself
because my body's in the way
Hidden door at last I see through
beyond dear body bag of bones
which I leave naked on a rock
Hidden door I wigless climb to
beyond that river
Hidden door at last I fall through
in the lost end of day
It is dusk
by the time we get to
Machu Picchu
Some Indians go by dancing
playing their flutes
and beating drums

(Peru-Chile, January-February, 1960)

HE

To Allen Ginsberg before "The Change"

He is one of the prophets come back
He is one of the wiggy prophets come back
He had a beard in the Old Testament
    but shaved it off in Paterson
He has a microphone around his neck
    at a poetry reading
    and he is more than one poet
    and he is an old man perpetually writing a poem
    about an old man
    whose every third thought is Death
    and who is writing a poem
    about an old man
    whose every third thought is Death
    and who is writing a poem
    Like the picture on a Quaker Oats box
    that shows a figure holding up a box
    upon which is a picture of a figure
    holding up a box

and the figure smaller and smaller
and further away each time
a picture of shrinking reality itself
He is one of the prophets come back
to see to hear to file a revised report
on the present state
of the shrinking world
He has buttonhooks in his eyes
with which he fastens on
to every foot of existence
and onto every shoestring rumor
of the nature of reality
And his eye fixes itself
on every stray person or thing
and waits for it to move
like a cat with a dead white mouse
suspecting it of hiding
some small clew to existence
and he waits gently
for it to reveal itself
or herself or himself
and he is gentle as the lamb of God
made into mad cutlets
And he picks up every suspicious object
and he picks up every person or thing
examining it and shaking it
like a white mouse with a piece of string
who thinks the thing is alive
and shakes it to speak
and shakes it alive
and shakes it to speak
He is a cat who creeps at night
and sleeps his buddhahood in the violet hour
and listens for the sound of three hands about to clap

and reads the script of his brainpan
his heiroglyph of existence
He is a talking asshole on a stick
    he is a walkie-talkie on two legs
    and he holds his phone to his ear
    and he holds his phone to his mouth
    and hears *Death death*
He has one head with one tongue hung
    in the back of his mouth
    and he speaks with an animal tongue
    and man has devised a language
    that no other animal understands
    and his tongue sees and his tongue speaks
    and his own ear hears what is said
    and clings to his head
    and hears *Death death*
    and he has a tongue to say it
    that no other animal understands
He is a forked root walking
    with a knot-hole eye in the middle of his head
    and his eye turns outward and inward
    and sees and is mad
    and is mad and sees
And he is the mad eye of the fourth person singular
    of which nobody speaks
    and he is the voice of the fourth person singular
    in which nobody speaks
    and which yet exists
    with a long head and a foolscap face
    and the long mad hair of death
    of which nobody speaks
And he speaks of himself and he speaks of the dead
    of his dead mother and his Aunt Rose

with their long hair and their long nails
that grow and grow
and they come back in his speech without a manicure
And he has come back with his black hair
and his black eye and his black shoes
and the big black book of his report
And he is a big black bird with one foot raised
to hear the sound of life reveal itself
on the shell of his sensorium
and he speaks to sing to get out of his skin
and he pecks with his tongue on the shell of it
and he knocks with his eye on the shell
and sees *light light* and hears *death death*
of which nobody speaks
For he is a head with a head's vision
and his is the lizard's look
and his unbuttoned vision is the door
in which he stands and waits and hears
the hand that knocks and claps and claps and knocks
his *Death Death*
For he is his own ecstatic illumination
and he is his own hallucination
and he is his own shrinker
and his eye turns in the shrinking head of the world
and hears his organ speak *Death Death*
a deaf music
For he has come at the end of the world
and he is the flippy flesh made word
and he speaks the word he hears in his flesh
and the word is *Death*

OVERPOPULATION

¿No se puede vivir sin amar?

I must have misunderstood something
in this story
There must be a misprint
in this paper
Hats off! It says here
The final war is over
again
Here they come again
parading by
the café terrace
I stand on my chair to see
I still can't see
the brave burned hero's face
I stand on the table
waving my only hat
with the hole in it
I throw the hole away
into the street
after the black limousine
I don't throw my paper
I sit down with my paper
which has the explanation of everything
except there's a hole in it
Something missing in the story
where the hole is

Or I must have misunderstood something
The nations have decided
it says here
to abolish themselves at last
It's been decided at the highest level
and at the lowest level
to return to a primitive society
For science has conquered nature
but nature must not be conquered
So science must be abolished
and machines must go
after all their turning and turning
The automobile is a passing thing
after all
The horse is here to stay
Population has reached its limit
There's standingroom only
Nowhere
to lie down
anymore
Medicine must be abolished
so people can die
when they're supposed to
There's still room
under the surface
I keep hoping
I have misunderstood something
in this story
People still lose
and find themselves
in bed
and animals still
aren't as cruel as people
because they can't talk
but we weren't designed

to live forever and ever
and design is everything
The little enzyme they've discovered
that causes aging
must be lost in the body again
All must be begun over
in a new pastoral era
There've been too many advances
Life can't bear it
any longer
Life is not a drug
made from mushrooms
eaten by Samoyeds in Siberia
which fully retain
their intoxicating properties
when transmitted in urine
so that an endless line of men
may get drunk over and over
on the same mushroom
a chain reaction of avid statues
with mouths at penises
I must have misunderstood something
in this story
Life is intoxicating
but can't go on and on
putting on more and more
complicated clothes
hats girdles garterbelts
uplift bras lifting higher and higher
until they fly away
and breasts fall
after all
We've got to get naked again
it says here
though fornication's still illegal

in certain states
I must have misunderstood something
in this story
The world's no Klee mobile
and there must be an end
to all this rotation
around the goofball sun
The sun in its sic transit
barely clears the rooftops now
bumps over a Mobilgas Pegasus
and sinks behind my paper
with its hole
in which I keep hoping
I've misunderstood something
for Death is not the answer
to our problem
There must be some mistake—
There is—
The editorials say
we must do something
and we cannot do anything
For something's missing
where the hole is
sitting on the terrace
of this fancy coffeehouse
on the left side of the world
where I must
have misunderstood something
as a purple blond sweeps by
and one too-high tit pops out
and falls in my plate
I return it to her
without looking too embarrassed
This she takes as a good sign
She sits down

and gives me the other
wrapped in silk
I go on reading my paper
thinking I must
have misunderstood something
trying to look like
it's all happened before
It has
It's a clay mobile
with something missing
where the hole is
I look under the table and see
our legs are intertwined
Our two chairs fuse
Our arms are round each other
She's facing me
crouched in my lap
her legs around me
My white snake has entered her
speaks of love inside of her
She moans to hear it
But
something's missing
Sex without love
wears gay deceivers
I still have one of her breasts
in my hand
The waiter comes running
picks up my fallen paper
hoping he's misunderstood something
None of us will ever die
as long as this goes on
The enzyme bottle
lies open
on the table

UNDERWEAR

I didn't get much sleep last night
thinking about underwear
Have you ever stopped to consider
underwear in the abstract
When you really dig into it
some shocking problems are raised
Underwear is something
we all have to deal with
Everyone wears
some kind of underwear
Even Indians
wear underwear
Even Cubans
wear underwear
The Pope wears underwear I hope
Underwear is worn by Negroes
The Governor of Louisiana
wears underwear
I saw him on TV
He must have had tight underwear
He squirmed a lot
Underwear can really get you in a bind
Negroes often wear
white underwear
which may lead to trouble
You have seen the underwear ads
for men and women
so alike but so different

Women's underwear holds things up
Men's underwear holds things down
Underwear is one thing
men and women have in common
Underwear is all we have between us
You have seen the three-color pictures
with crotches encircled
to show the areas of extra strength
and three-way stretch
promising full freedom of action
Don't be deceived
It's all based on the two-party system
which doesn't allow much freedom of choice
the way things are set up
America in its Underwear
struggles thru the night
Underwear controls everything in the end
Take foundation garments for instance
They are really fascist forms
of underground government
making people believe
something but the truth
telling you what you can or can't do
Did you ever try to get around a girdle
Perhaps Non-Violent Action
is the only answer
Did Gandhi wear a girdle?
Did Lady Macbeth wear a girdle?
Was that why Macbeth murdered sleep?
And that spot she was always rubbing—
Was it really in her underwear?
Modern anglosaxon ladies
must have huge guilt complexes
always washing and washing and washing
Out damned spot—rub don't blot—

Underwear with spots very suspicious
Underwear with bulges very shocking
Underwear on clothesline a great flag of freedom
Someone has escaped his Underwear
May be naked somewhere
Help!
But don't worry
Everybody's still hung up in it
There won't be no real revolution
And poetry still the underwear of the soul
And underwear still covering
a multitude of faults
in the geological sense—
strange sedimentary stones, inscrutable cracks!
And that only the beginning
For does not the body stay alive
after death
and still need its underwear
or outgrow it
some organs said to reach full maturity
only after the head stops holding them back?
If I were you I'd keep aside
an oversize pair of winter underwear
Do not go naked into that good night
And in the meantime
keep calm and warm and dry
No use stirring ourselves up prematurely
'over Nothing'
Move forward with dignity
hand in vest
Don't get emotional
And death shall have no dominion
There's plenty of time my darling
Are we not still young and easy
Don't shout

come lie with me and be my love

Come lie with me and be my love

Love lie with me

Lie down with me

Under the cypress tree

In the sweet grasses

Where the wind lieth

Where the wind dieth

As night passes

Come lie with me

All night with me

And have enough of kissing me

And have enough of making love

And let my lizard speak to thee

And let our two selves speak

All night under the cypress tree

Without making love

THE GREAT CHINESE DRAGON

The great Chinese dragon which is the greatest dragon in all the
world and which once upon a time was towed across the
Pacific by a crew of coolies rowing in an open boat—was
the first real live dragon ever actually to reach these shores
And the great Chinese dragon passing thru the Golden Gate
spouting streams of water like a string of fireboats then broke
loose somewhere near China Camp gulped down a hundred
Chinese seamen and forthwith ate up all the shrimp in San
Francisco Bay
And the great Chinese dragon was therefore forever after confined
in a Chinatown basement and ever since allowed out only for
Chinese New Year's parades and other Unamerican demon-
strations paternally watched-over by those benevolent men in
blue who represent our more advanced civilization which has
reached such a high state of democracy as to allow even a
few barbarians to carry on their quaint native customs in our
midst
And thus the great Chinese dragon which is the greatest dragon
in all the world now can only be seen creeping out of an
Adler Alley cellar like a worm out of a hole sometime during
the second week in February every year when it sorties out
of hibernation in its Chinese storeroom pushed from behind
by a band of fortythree Chinese electricians and technicians
who stuff its peristaltic accordion-body up thru a sidewalk
delivery entrance

And first the swaying snout appears and then the eyes at ground level feeling along the curb and then the head itself casting about and swaying and heaving finally up to the corner of Grant Avenue itself where a huge paper sign proclaims the *World's Largest Chinatown*

And the great Chinese dragon's jaws wired permanently agape as if by a demented dentist to display the Cadmium teeth as the hungry head heaves out into Grant Avenue right under the sign and raising itself with a great snort of fire suddenly proclaims the official firecracker start of the Chinese New Year

And the lightbulb eyes lighting up and popping out on coiled wire springs and the body stretching and rocking further and further around the corner and down Grant Avenue like a caterpillar rollercoaster with the eyes sprung out and waving in the air like the blind feelers of some mechanical preying mantis and the eyes blinking on and off with Chinese red pupils and tiny bamboo-blind eyelids going up and down

And still the tail of the dragon in the Adler Alley cellar uncoiling and unwinding out into the street with the fortythree Chinese technicians still stuffing the dragon out the hole in the sidewalk and the head of the dragon now three blocks away in the middle of the parade of fancy floats presided over by Chinese virgins

And here comes the St. Mary's Chinese Girls' Drum Corps and here come sixteen white men in pith helmets beating big bass drums representing the Order of the Moose and here comes a gang of happy car salesmen disguised as Islam Shriners and here comes a chapter of the Order of Improved Red Men and here comes a cordon of motorcycle cops in crash helmets with radios going followed by a small papier-mâché lion fed with Nekko wafers and run by two guys left over from a Ten-Ten festival which in turn is followed by the great Chinese dragon itself gooking over balconies as it comes

And the great Chinese dragon has eaten a hundred humans and
their legs pop out of his underside and are his walking legs
which are not mentioned in the official printed program in
which he is written up as the Great Golden Dragon made in
Hong Kong to the specifications of the Chinese Chamber of
Commerce and he represents the force and mystery of life
and his head sways in the sky between the balconies as he
comes followed by six Chinese boy scouts wearing Keds and
carrying strings of batteries that light up the dragon like a
nighttime freeway

And he has lain all winter among a heap of collapsed paper
lanterns and green rubber lizards and ivory backscratchers
with the iron sidewalk doors closed over his head but he has
now sprung up with the first sign of Spring like the force of
life itself and his head sways in the sky and gooks in green
windows as he comes

And he is a monster with the head of a dog and the body of a
serpent risen yearly out of the sea to devour a virgin thrown
from a cliff to appease him and he is a young man handsome
and drunk ogling the girls and he has high ideals and a
hundred sport shoes and he says No to Mother and he is a
big red table the world will never tilt and he has big eyes
everywhere thru which he sees all womankind milkwhite and
dove-breasted and he will eat their waterflowers for he is the
cat with future feet wearing Keds and he eats cake out of
pastry windows and is hungrier and more potent and more
powerful and more omnivorous than the papier-mâché lion
run by two guys and he is the great earthworm of lucky life
filled with flowing Chinese semen and he considers his own
and our existence in its most profound sense as he comes and
he has no Christian answer to the existential question even
as he sees the spiritual everywhere translucent in the material
world and he does not want to escape the responsibility of

being a dragon or the consequences of his long horny tail still buried in the basement but the blue citizens on their talking cycles think that he wants to escape and at all costs he must not be allowed to escape because the great Chinese dragon is the greatest potential dragon in all the world and if allowed to escape from Chinatown might gallop away up their new freeway at the Broadway entrance mistaking it for a Great Wall of China or some other barbarian barrier and so go careening along it chewing up stanchions and signposts and belching forth some strange disintegrating medium which might melt down the great concrete walls of America and they are afraid of how far the great Chinese dragon might really go starting from San Francisco and so they have secretly and securely tied down the very end of his tail in its hole

  so that

     this great pulsing phallus of life at the very end of its parade at the very end of Chinatown gives one wild orgasm of a shudder and rolls over fainting in the bright night street since even for a dragon every orgasm is a little death

And then the great Chinese dragon starts silently shrinking and shriveling up and drawing back and back and back to its first cave and the soft silk skin wrinkles up and shrinks and shrinks on its sprung bamboo bones and the handsome dejected head hangs down like a defeated prizefighter's and so is stuffed down again at last into its private place and the cellar sidewalk doors press down again over the great wilted head with one small hole of an eye blinking still thru the gratings of the metal doors as the great Chinese dragon gives one last convulsive earthquake shake and rolls over dead-dog to wait another white year for the final coming and the final sowing of his oats and teeth

TENTATIVE DESCRIPTION OF A DINNER TO PROMOTE THE IMPEACHMENT OF PRESIDENT EISENHOWER

After it became obvious that the strange rain would never stop
And after it became obvious that the President was doing every-
    thing in his power
And after it became obvious that the President's general staff was
    still in contact with the President deep in the heart of Georgia
    while deep in the heart of South America the President's
    left-hand man was proving all the world loves an American
And after it became obvious that the strange rain would never
    stop and that Old Soldiers never drown and that roses in the
    rain had forgotten the word for bloom and that perverted
    pollen blown on sunless seas was eaten by irradiated fish who
    spawned up cloudleaf streams and fell onto our dinnerplates
And after it became obvious that the President was doing every-
    thing in his power to make the world safe for nationalism his
    brilliant military mind never having realized that nationalism
    itself was the idiotic superstition which would blow up the
    world
And after it became obvious that the President nevertheless still
    carried no matter where he went in the strange rain the little
    telegraph key which like a can opener could be used instantly
    to open but not to close the hot box of final war if not to

waylay any stray asinine action by any stray asinine second
lieutenant pressing any strange button anywhere far away
over an arctic ocean thus illuminating the world once and
for all

And after it became obvious that the law of gravity was still in
effect and that what blows up must come down on everyone
including white citizens

And after it became obvious that the Voice of America was really
the Deaf Ear of America and that the President was unable
to hear the underprivileged natives of the world shouting No
Contamination Without Representation in the strange rain
from which there was no escape—except Peace

And after it became obvious that the word Truth had only a comic
significance to the Atomic Energy Commission while the
President danced madly to mad Admiral Straus waltzes wear-
ing special atomic earplugs which prevented him from hearing
Albert Schweitzer and nine thousand two hundred and thirty-
five other scientists telling him about spastic generations and
blind boneless babies in the strange rain from which there was
no escape—except Peace

And after it became obvious that the President was doing every-
thing in his power to get thru the next four years without
eating any of the crates of irradiated vegetables wellwishers
had sent him from all over and which were filling the corri-
dors and antechambers and bedchambers and chamberpots in
the not-so-White House

And after it became obvious that the Great Soldier had become
the Great Conciliator who had become the Great Com-
promiser who had become the Great Fence Sitter who actu-
ally had heard of the Supreme Court's decision to desegregate
the land of the free and had not only heard of it but had
actually

read it

And after it became obvious that the President had gone to Gettysburg fourscore and seven years ago and had given his Gettysburg Address to the postman and so dedicated himself to the unfinished task

Then it was that the natives of the Republic began assembling in the driving rain from which there was no escape—except Peace

And then it was that no invitations had to be sent out for the great testimonial dinner except to politicians whose respected names would lend weight to the project but who did not come anyway suspecting the whole thing was a plot to save the world from the clean bomb from which there was no escape—except Peace

And women who still needed despair to look truly tragic came looking very beautiful and very tragic indeed since there was despair to spare

And some men also despaired and sat down in Bohemia and were too busy to come

But other men came whose only political action during the past twenty years had been to flush a protesting toilet and run

And babies came in their carriages carrying irradiated dolls and holding onto crazy strings of illuminated weather balloons filled with Nagasaki air

And those who had not left their TV sets long enough to notice the weather in seven years now came swimming thru the rain holding their testimonials

And those came who had never marched in sports car protest parades and those came who had never been arrested for sailing a protesting Golden Rule in unpacific oceans

And Noah came in his own Ark looking surprisingly like an outraged Jesus Christ and cruised about flying his pinion and picking up two of each beast that wanted to be preserved in the strange rain which was raining real cats and dogs and from which there was no escape—except Peace

And peddlers came in lead jockstraps selling hotdogs and rubber American flags and waving petitions proclaiming it Unamerican to play golf on the same holy days that clean bombs were set off on time

And finally after everyone who was anyone and after everyone who was no one had arrived and after every soul was seated and waiting for the symbolic mushroom soup to be served and for the keynote speeches to begin

The President himself came in

Took one look around and said

We Resign

(May, 1958)

SPECIAL CLEARANCE SALE OF FAMOUS MASTERPIECES

It was a crazy scene to hitch-hike into
    what with all of it taking place
    on one small ball of earth
    like some kind of work-in-progress
    by some puttyball sculptor
    or nightmaze novelist
Yes it was a crazy scene to hitch-hike into
    like lighting on a Rand McNally globe
    with compass roses looking like real islands
    and trees towers telephones
    bridges bedsprings rivers
    fountains and crosses
    sprouting up out of it
    as it whirls around
    disgorging strings of colored lights
    rockets popbottles candy and cigarettes
    like an enormous IBM automat hung in space
    and run by solar energy
And all of it held together with light and bones
    and roots and mud and bubblegum and tar
    and jass and spit and skin and reinforced concrete
    and skeins of yarn and clotheslines
    and hope and clay

And the whole scene turning and turning
    through the soundless wigless air
    like some huge store-window carousel
    with a Special Clearance Sale of Famous Masterpieces
Including one replica of Rodin's Thinker with hand on chin
    pondering the insoluble problem
    next to one bronze head of Albert Einstein
    next to a megaphone mask of a Muse of Tragedy
    pondering the insoluble problem
    next to a fragment of a medieval crucifix
    with the painted wood head of Christ
    pondering the insoluble problem
    next to a biblical painting of Adam
    sitting under a denuded figtree with hand on chin
    and one rib missing and a bitten apple in his hand
    for the first time pondering the insoluble problem
    next to a painted bust of Queen Nefertiti
    with blind eyes pondering the insoluble problem
    next to one Venus de Milo
    next to one Mona Lisa
    next to Whistler's Mother
    next to one white Unicorn in Captivity
    next to a wooden model of the Trojan Horse
    with clay men inside with hands on chin
    pondering the insoluble problem
    next to a watercolor Jonah inside his whale
    next to a rubber working model of Moby Dick
    with Ahab on his back
    with one leg missing and hand on chin
    pondering the insoluble problem
    next to a gift edition of Shakespeare
    open to an illustration of Hamlet
    with chinless Yorick in his hand

pondering the insoluble problem
next to a cardboard Lincoln Memoiral
with Lincoln inside
pondering the insoluble problem
next to a painting of Washington Crossing the Delaware
standing in the boat against Navy Regulations
and attempting to look like he's pondering
the insoluble problem
next to one Potsdam Souvenir Photo
of Churchill Roosevelt and Stalin
one of whom is pondering the insoluble problem
next to a hollow Buddha with holes in head
through which incense smokes
above and beyond and behind the insoluble problem
next to one marked-down
                    Picasso Peace Dove
        turning and turning
                        on a roasting spit
                                    of burning air
        upon which also turn and burn and burn
                                        and burn
                                        and burn
                                        and burn
                all kinds of still segregated
                            screaming human
                        animals
                with varying numbers of
                            charred chins
                            skinless breasts
                            and charcoal cocks

    in a final insoluble solution
    to the insoluble problem

ONE THOUSAND FEARFUL WORDS FOR FIDEL CASTRO

I am sitting in Mike's Place trying to figure out
what's going to happen
without Fidel Castro
Among the salami sandwiches and spittoons
I see no solution
It's going to be a tragedy
I see no way out
among the admen and slumming models
and the brilliant snooping columnists
who are qualified to call Castro psychotic
because they no doubt are doctors
and have examined him personally
and know a paranoid hysterical tyrant when they see one
because they have it on first hand
from personal observation by the CIA
and the great disinterested news services
And Hearst is dead but his great Cuban wire still stands:
"You get the pictures, I'll make the War"
I see no answer
I see no way out
among the paisanos playing pool
it looks like Curtains for Fidel
They're going to fix his wagon
in the course of human events

In the back of Mike's the pinball machines
shudder and leap from the floor
when Cuban Charlie shakes them
and tries to work his will
on one named "Independence Sweepstakes"
Each pinball wandered lonely as a man
siphons thru and sinks
no matter how he twists and turns
A billiardball falls in a felt pocket
like a peasant in a green landscape
You're whirling around in your little hole
Fidel
and you'll soon sink
in the course of human events

On the nickelodeon a cowboy ballad groans
"Got myself a Cadillac" the cowhand moans
He didn't get it in Cuba, baby
Outside in the night of North Beach America
the new North American cars flick by
from Motorama
their headlights never bright enough
to dispel this night
in the course of human events

Three creepy men come in
One is Chinese
One is Negro
One is some kind of crazy Indian
They look like they may have been
walking up and down in Cuba
but they haven't
All three have hearing aids

It's a little deaf brotherhood of Americans
The skinny one screws his hearing aid
in his skinny ear
He's also got a little transistor radio
the same size as his hearing aid box
For a moment I confuse the two

The radio squawks
some kind of memorial program:
"When in the course of human events
it becomes necessary for one people
to dissolve the political bonds
which have connected them with another—"
I see no way out
no escape
He's tuned in on your frequency, Fidel
but can't hear it
There's interference
It's going to be
a big evil tragedy
They're going to fix you, Fidel
with your big Cuban cigar
which you stole from us
and your army surplus hat
which you probably also stole
and your Beat beard

History may absolve you, Fidel
but we'll dissolve you first, Fidel
You'll be dissolved in history
We've got the solvent
We've got the chaser
and we'll have a little party

somewhere down your way, Fidel
It's going to be a Gas
As they say in Guatemala

Outside of Mike's Place now
an ambulance sirens up
It's a midnight murder or something
Some young bearded guy stretched on the sidewalk
with blood sticking out
Here's your little tragedy, Fidel
They're coming to pick you up
and stretch you on their Stretcher
That's what happens, Fidel
when in the course of human events
it becomes necessary for one people to dissolve
the bonds of International Tel & Tel
and United Fruit
Fidel
How come you don't answer anymore
Fidel
Did they cut you off our frequency
We've closed down our station anyway
We've turned you off, Fidel

I was sitting in Mike's place, Fidel
waiting for someone else to act
like a good Liberal
I hadn't quite finished reading Camus' *Rebel*
so I couldn't quite recognize you, Fidel
walking up and down your island
when they came for you, Fidel
"My Country or Death" you told them
Well you've got your little death, Fidel

like old Honest Abe
one of your boyhood heroes
who also had his little Civil War
and was a different kind of Liberator
(since no one was shot in his war)
and also was murdered
in the course of human events

Fidel . . . Fidel . . .
your coffin passes by
thru lanes and streets you never knew
thru day and night, Fidel
While lilacs last in the dooryard bloom, Fidel
your futile trip is done
yet is not done
and is not futile
I give you my sprig of laurel

San Francisco, January, 1961

BERLIN

A song a line a free phrase
keeps recurring
Under the Linden trees . . .
Under the Linden trees . . .
As if everything had begun over
as if I had it to do
all over
here where I'm still walking & looking
for the great indelible poem
Where is it gone
Is it here in Woolworth's
A stickysweet candysmell
fills the air
Perhaps they're spraying it
through Woolworth's ventilators
a kind of chemical warfare
hits you on the sidewalk
It sucks you in
into the soft machine
I'm suffocating
in this gucky smell
Is this like dying
inside an amoeba
everything soft & warm & squishy
I'm already being digested
inside Woolworth's
Mother I'm in you again

I'm being sucked down that whirlpool
of pinkcotton candy
which that Circe spins
by the revolving door
which revolves around me
winding me around it
as in the gooey funnel
a sticky wicket I'm stuck in
reminds me of Berlin
Must be some moving sidewalk
flypaper escalator
sweeping people in
shoes stuck to it
Otherwise they'd never get so many
I had not known
life had undone so many
inside Woolworth's sweet machine
Put in a slug
out comes your weight with your fate
in a cardboard heroic couplet
I'm still looking for my poem
I am looking for a great refrain
I've tried fortune cookies
and found them empty
despite the Chinese sages
imprisoned in cooky factories
For a while I contemplated a plot
to infiltrate the Chinese Fortune Cooky Industry
A real underground for San Francisco poets
It would have worked
if only the Chinese printer
hadn't pied our fortunes
claiming they were Inscrutable
and all looked alike to him

So I'm reduced to Greater Woolworth's
a microcosm of sweet America
What a scene
Fantastic display of
soft toothbrushes
herds of women
Sweet valley where I sing my song
of free enterprise
(Think what Thorstein Veblen thought
when he first spied it
from a rise)
Is there a poem here
Is it worth saving
Solitary
singing in the West
I strike up for a New World
Where is the song gone
where is my poem
I may have no more poetry
but I still have my Poetics
like certain elder poets
Poetics are the politics of poetry
sticking feet to flypaper
making everything and everyone
hang together
but I like live models
like all those free feet at dog level
Unter den Linden
I have a German friend
who writes hard poetry
He often accompanies me
to Greater Woolworth's
It's not like this in the East Zone
At one soft counter we come upon

a new German invention
a kind of Cor-recto-type paper
on which you simply type
the same mistake again
in the exact same place
and the paper erases
the original sin
by a kind of chemical amnesia
Ain't that ingenious
ain't that great
Two wrongs make a right in Berlin
Unter den Linden
by Brandenburg Gate
as if everything had begun over
as if we had it to do all over
as when my mother held me
on a lovely balcony
and waved my hand for me
at another grand parade
(How wonderful to think
God loved us
if we prayed)

Am I to keep waving
When will it begin
Where is my lyrik
where is my epic
who erased it
Unter den Linden
I lost it somewhere
other side of the sun
a love poem I had begun
where gone dumb poem
wrought from the dark in my mother long ago

Ah but
the Rhine maidens
still are singing
And "underneath the lamplight Lily Marlene"
Dumb siren song!
Die Walkyrie!
Die Meistersinger!
Steppenwulf I see you!
Sophisticated weapons!
Weapons-delivery systems!
Welcome back, General Clay!

God, come back, Innocence of the World
a song a line a free phrase
in autumn capitals
their avenues of leaves ablaze

Prisoners of history
bound hand and foot!
we weep to hear again
those sirens sing again
over the wrong rivers

where all those feet again
tap to march in measure again
to the rhythm of typewriter keys
by blind touchtypists
A typed line a chant a great refrain—
Their poem, not mine
while still in Spring the cuckoo cries and cries
and cries again. . . .

THE SITUATION in the WEST followed by a Holy Proposal

Kyrie Eleison Kerista

Dreaming of utopias
where everyone's a lover
I see San Francisco from my window
thru some old navy beerbottles
The glass is dark
What's it all about
I move the ships about
in my binoculars
like some mad admiral
Dark Dark Dark
we are all shunted into it
a concrete Crete
freeway pinball labyrinth
cars into tunnels
dancers long gone under the hills
kiss kiss in stone boudoirs
the earth a turbine
storing sexual energy
turning and turning into the dark
under the skyscrapers with their time on top
tickertape time tick tick
civilization and its crickets
The dark thread

draws us all in
into the wind-up labyrinth
undischarged sexual energy
not mine the city's
There's the Fairmont phallus
There's the Mark masturbation
There's the Park there's the cement works
There's the Steam Beer Brewing Plant
There's the Actor's Workshop
Nothing brewing there these days
There's the Bay there's that Bridge
There's that treasured Island the Navy doesn't need
We need it but we don't need the Navy
Sail Away forever somewhere why don't you
Ah there's the sun again
There's the Hall of Justice blockhouse
personifying itself
Mussolini Modern
There's the sky there's skywriting
chalk on a mirror
What's it all about
Someone trying to trace something up there
Sun solves it
in the mirror
of eternity
A train pulls out of Third Street Station
not going anywhere
discharge of aimless sexual energy
tick tick over the rails
to a coupling in Palo Alto
Life goes on not going anywhere
Time goes on tick tick
what's it all about

find the tick in the labyrêve
of eternity
follow your thread
around the next corner
I sometimes wonder if that is what Krishnamurti meant
Love's a lost tick and desire fails
As we grow older the clatter becomes more complicated
Put your ear to the flesh and you'll still hear it
tick tick over the rails
bearing us away
And there is a time to die
and there is a time to live
but who's got a bad ticker
and what's everything waiting for
Don't tell me they're still Waiting
We've been thru all that already
even the poets dug it
you could almost hear them beginning to think
tick tick
even the painters finally caught on pop pop
Now it's all over maybe
nothing happening anyplace anymore maybe
especially in San Francisco baby
stranded whales all over the place
elder statesmen poets high and dry
flopping about out of breath
and a labyrinth the worst place of all
for a whale to find himself
How do we get out
where do we go from here
what's the next development
what's around the next corner
why is everything holding its breath

why am I here typing
turned-on in my attic
holding my breath Om Om
tick tick
I've got a good ticker
I'm winding up my thread
but I am no Prince Theseus nor was meant to be
I'll slay no minotaurs in my Attic retreat
with the sword I use to cut my meat
Still I'm always looking for the action
at the heart of things
Must be something shaking somewhere
someone on some rooftop must be loving
in the hot sun
in this labyrinth of solitude
which is neither cold Crete nor hot Mexico
but is still full of solos
gringo pachucos
trying to trace it out
trying to figure out
what it's all about
and why the sun still goes on turning
and still is god to my dog
The sun the sun behold the sun
Great God Sun still riseth
in our rubaiyat
and strikes the towers with a shaft of light
The sun the sun still rules everything
even the sky as we know it
even love as we know it
even life which is nothing but heat
discharge of sexual energy
And there is a time to embrace

and there is a time to refrain from embracing
and the sun goes on cooling
Discharge of undirected sexual energy
and the Cold War gets cooler and desire fails
Other-directed sexual energy
And there is a time to hate
and there is a time to love
and there is a time to keep silence
and there is a time to speak
and two more government scientists throw in the sponge
Mis-directed sexual energy
But is this cooling-off period to string us out forever
How about some love in the cool-cool climate
how about some instant joy
inner-directed sexual energy
let's get hot again baby
I didn't say Shoot I said Fuck
I'm sorry officer don't take me away
I'm sorry Mother
that's the only word that works
It's a word of love daddy
for which there's no refined substitute
even in French
Still I'm trying to refine it
I'm trying to make it holy
I'm trying to make it socially acceptable
even to Cretan cretins lost in a maze
for to fuck is to love again
and we shall rise up again at the voice of a bird
and there is a time to hate
and there is a time to love
so let's everybody love it up
in the sun
which won't burn on forever and ever

That's the solution Comrade
maybe the only one Comrade
Why are you so puritanical Comrade
kicking Allen Ginsberg out of Czechoslovakia
Let's turn on together Comrade
and you too Colonel Cornpone
I'm serious Comrade
I'm serious Colonel Cornpone
let's repeat it together
To fuck is to love again
kyrie eleison hallelujah
A litany like that
means more to us Romans
than any Hail Mary full of grace
though blessed be the fruit of her womb
And don't think you have to lie down abjectly General
for there is a time to kill
and there is a time to kiss
but the tick of hate is loose in the labyrinth
dies irae dies illa illa illa
and ticks carry diseases but kisses carry love
which is also infectious
And there is a time for war
and there is a time for a piece of love
So get ready General
Ready Get Set Fuck
kyrie kyrie hallelujah
By the right flank Fuck
and blessed be the fruit
By the left flank Fuck
and blessed be the fruit
By the rear Fuck
Blessed Blessed Blessed
So kiss thy neighbor in another country

kyrie kyrie kyrie
exchange fucking populations
kyrie kyrie hallelujah
You send us all your women in babushkas
We'll send you all our men wearing neckties
Americans love travel
We love exotic places and people
We dig Chinese chicks we dig Cuban chicks we dig Arab boys
You'll think ours are exotic too
I'm tired of this climate anyway
you're tired of yours
so let's get together on this
let's get down to bare essentials
and have a mass exchange fuck
a fucking real exchange program
an enormous international hardcore Fuck Corps
And nevermind the protocol
and nevermind the quotas
We've all got our own passe-partout
if to fuck is to love again
And nevermind the overpopulation
Contraception can contain
all but love
And blessed be the fruit of transcopulation
and blessed be the fruit of transpopulation
and blessed be the fucking world with no more nations!
hosanna pulchrissima
kyrie kyrie kyrie kyrie hallelujah!
we'll all still have the sun
in which to recognize ourselves at last across the world
over the obscene boundaries!

San Francisco-London 1964–65
Read at Royal Albert Hall, London, June 11, 1965